**WHO
ARE
WE
NOW?**

Selected Works by Lawrence Ferlinghetti

POETRY

Pictures of the Gone World (City Lights Books, 1955)
A Coney Island of the Mind (New Directions, 1958)
Translation: Jacques Prévert, *Paroles*
(City Lights Books, 1958)
Starting from San Francisco (New Directions, 1967)
The Secret Meaning of Things (New Directions, 1968)
Back Roads to Far Places (New Directions, 1971)
Open Eye, Open Heart (New Directions, 1973)
Who Are We Now? (New Directions, 1976)

PROSE

Her (New Directions, 1960)
Tyrannus Nix? (New Directions, 1969)
The Mexican Night (New Directions, 1970)

PLAYS

Unfair Arguments with Existence (New Directions, 1963)
Routines (New Directions, 1964)

FILMS

Have You Sold Your Dozen Roses? (1960)
Tyrannus Nix? (N.E.T., 1969)
Assassination Raga, with Max Crosley (1973)

RECORDINGS

Poetry Readings in "The Cellar," with Kenneth Rexroth
(Fantasy LP7002, 1958)
*Tentative Description of a Dinner to Impeach
President Eisenhower & Other Poems* (Fantasy LP7004, 1959)
The World's Great Poets, Volume 1, with Allen Ginsberg
and Gregory Corso, Spoleto Festival, 1965
(CMS LP617, 1971)
Tyrannus Nix? & Assassination Raga (Fantasy LP7014, 1971)

LAWRENCE FERLINGHETTI

WHO
ARE
WE
NOW?

A NEW DIRECTIONS BOOK

Manufactured in the United States of America
First published clothbound and as New Directions Paperbook 425 in 1976
Published simultaneously in Canada by McClelland & Stewart, Ltd.

Library of Congress Cataloging in Publication Data

Ferlinghetti, Lawrence.
  Who are we now?

  (A New Directions Book)
  I. Title.
PS3511.E557W5   811'.5'4   76–10681
ISBN 0–8112–0628–9
ISBN 0–8112–0629–7 pbk.

New Directions Books are published for James Laughlin
by New Directions Publishing Corporation,
333 Sixth Avenue, New York 10014

THIRD PRINTING

CONTENTS

"Underneath all art and social life, sex and fraternity"
        —Edward Carpenter, *Days with Walt Whitman*

THE JACK OF HEARTS
(For Dylan)

Who are we now, who are we ever,
Skin books parchment bodies libraries of the living
gilt almanachs of the very rich
encyclopedias of little people
packs of players face down
on faded maps of America
with no Jack of Hearts
in the time of the ostrich
Fields full of rooks
dumb pawns in black-and-white kingdoms
And revolutions the festivals of the oppressed
and festivals the little revolutions
of the bourgeoisie
where gypsy fortune tellers deal
without the Jack of Hearts
the black-eyed one who sees all ways
the one with the eye of a horse
the one with the light in his eye
the one with his eye on the star named Nova
the one for the ones with no one to lead them
the one whose day has just begun
the one with the star in his cap
the cat with future feet
looking like a Jack of Hearts
mystic Jack Zen Jack with crazy koans
Vegas Jack who rolls the bones
the high roller behind the dealer
the one who'll shake them
the one who'll shake the ones unshaken
the fearless one

1

the one without bullshit
the stud with the straightest answer
the one with blazing words for guns
the distance runner with the word to pass
the night rider with the urgent message
The man from La Mancha riding bareback
The one who bears the great tradition
and breaks it
The Mysterious Stranger who comes & goes
The Jack of Hearts who speaks out
in the time of the ostrich
the one who sees the ostrich
the one who sees what the ostrich sees in the sand
the one who digs the mystery
and stands in the corner smiling
like a Jack of Hearts
at the ones with no one to lead them
the ones with their eyes in the sands
the sand that runs through the glass
the ones who don't want to look
at what's going down around them
the shut-eye ones who wish
that someone else would seize the day
that someone else would tell them
which way up and which way out
and whom to hate and whom to love
like Big Jack groovy Jack the Jack of light
Sainted Jack who had the Revelations
and spoke the poem of apocalypse
Poet Jack with the light pack
who travels by himself
and leaves the ladies smiling
Dharma Jack with the beatitudes
drunk on a bus addressing everyone
the silent ones with the frozen faces

the ones with *The Wall Street Journal*
who never speak to strangers
the ones that got lost in the shuffle
and never drew the Jack of Hearts
the one who'd turn them on
who'd save them from themselves
the one who heals the Hamlet in them
the silent Ham who never acts
like the Jack of Hearts
the dude on the corner in two-tone shoes
who knows the name of the game
and names his game
the kid who paints the fence
the boy who digs the treasure up
the boy with the beans on the beanstalk
the dandy man the candy man
the one with the lollipops
the harlequin man
who tells the tic-toc man to stuff it
in front of the house that Jack built
behind the house that Jack built
where sleeps the Cock that crowed in the morn
where sleeps the Cow with the crumpled horn
where sleeps the dude who kept the horse
with the beautiful form
and kissed the Maiden all forlorn
the Jack of the pack all tattered and torn
the one the queen keeps her eye on
Dark Rider on a white horse
after the Apocalypse
Prophet stoned on the wheel of fortune
Sweet singer with harp half-hid
who speaks with the cry of cicadas
who tells the tale too truly
for the ones with no one to tell them

the true tale of sound and fury
the Jack of Hearts who lays it out
who tells it as it is
the one who wears no watch
yet tells the time too truly
and reads the Knight of Cups
and knows himself
the Knave of Hearts the Jack of Hearts
who stole the tarts
of love & laughter
the Jack who tells his dream
to those with no one to dream it
the one who tells his dream
to the hard-eyed innocents
and lays it out for the blind hippie
the black dream the white dream
of the Jack of Hearts
whose skeleton is neither black nor white
the long dream the dream of heads & hearts
the trip of hearts the flip of hearts
that turns the Hanged Man right side up
and saves the Drowned Sailor
with the breath of love
the wet dream the hard dream the sweet dream
of the Deck Hand on the tall ship sailing softly
Blackjack yellowjack the steeplejack
who sets the clock in the tower
and sees the chimes of freedom flashing
his only watch within him
the high one the turned-on one the tuned-in one
the one who digs
in the time of the ostrich
and finds the sun-stone
of himself

the woman-man
the whole man
who holds all worlds together
when all is said and all is done
in the wild eye the wide eye
of the Jack of Hearts
who stands in a doorway
clothed in sun

DIRECTOR OF ALIENATION

Looking in the mirrors at Macy's
and thinking it's a subterranean plot
to make me feel like Chaplin
snuck in with his bent shoes & beat bowler
looking for a fair-haired angel
Who's this bum
crept in off the streets
blinking in the neon
an anarchist among the floorwalkers
a strike-breaker even
right past the pickets
and the picket line is the People yet?
I think I'll hook a new derby
with my cane
and put a sign on it reading
Director of Alienation
or The Real Revolution
So it's Mister Alienation is it
like he don't like nobody?
It's not me It's Them out of step
I came in looking for an angel
male or female dark or fair
but why does everyone look
so serious or unhappy
like as if everyone's alienated
from something or someone
from the whole earth even
and the green land
among the loud indignant birds
My land is your land
but 'all is changed, changed utterly'

Look at this alien face
in this elevator mirror
The Tele-tector scans me
He looks paranoid Better get him out
before he starts trying on the underwear
Keep your filthy mitts offa
I better stick to the escalators
Too many nylon ladies in the lifts
too many two-way mirrors
I came in looking for an angel
among the alien corn
I might get caught
fingering the lingerie
feeling up the manikins
House dicks after me
Where's your credit cards
They'll find the hole in my sock
in the Shoe Department
The full-length mirrors all designed
to make you look your worst
so you'll get real depressed
and throw off your old clothes
and buy new duds on the spot
Well I'll take them at their word
They asked for it
Off with these grungy threads
and slide down the escalators bare-ass
Slip between the on-sale sheets
into the on-sale bed
feeling for an angel in it
Try this new flush toilet
and the portable shower
emerging from the bath in something sexy
into a store window
among the Coquette Wigs by Eva Gabor

and freeze in one of the wigs
when the Keystone Cops come running
I came in looking for an angel
passion eyes and longing hair
in mirrors made of water
But what's this wrack of civilization
I've fallen into
This must be the end of something
the last days of somebody's empire
Seven floors of it
from Women's Wear to Men's Furnishings
Lost souls descending thru
Dante's seven circles
Ladies like bees avaricious
clustered at counters
I don't want to join them either
Always the Outsider
What a drag
Why don't you get with it
It's your country
What a cliché this Outsider
a real bore
But is there anyone left inside
in this year of the boring Bicentennial
Indians alienated Artists alienated
All these poets alienated
Parents husbands wives alienated
Kids alienated
Even billionaires alienated
hiding out in foreign countries
Don't let them tell you different
with their flags and their grants
So Buy Buy Buy
and get Inside
Get a loada this junk

You wanna belong
You gotta have it
Pull yourself together
and descend to Macy's basement
And eat your way up
thru the seven stages
of this classless society
with the Credit Department on the top floor
where surely some revelation is at hand
Consume your way up
until you're consumed by it
at the very top
where surely a terrible beauty is born
Then jump off the roof
o dark of hair
o Ruth among the alien corn
waving plastic jewels and genitals

WILD DREAMS OF A NEW BEGINNING

There's a breathless hush on the freeway tonight
Beyond the ledges of concrete
restaurants fall into dreams
with candlelight couples
Lost Alexandria still burns
in a billion lightbulbs
Lives cross lives
idling at stoplights
Beyond the cloverleaf turnoffs
'Souls eat souls in the general emptiness'
A piano concerto comes out a kitchen window
A yogi speaks at Ojai
'It's all taking place in one mind'
On the lawn among the trees
lovers are listening
for the master to tell them they are one
with the universe
Eyes smell flowers and become them
There's a deathless hush
on the freeway tonight
as a Pacific tidal wave a mile high
                              sweeps in

Los Angeles breathes its last gas
and sinks into the sea like the *Titanic* all lights lit
Nine minutes later Willa Cather's Nebraska
                              sinks with it

The seas come in over Utah
Mormon tabernacles washed away like barnacles
Coyotes are confounded & swim nowhere
An orchestra onstage in Omaha
keeps on playing Handel's *Water Music*
Horns fill with water

and bass players float away on their instruments
clutching them like lovers horizontal
Chicago's Loop becomes a rollercoaster
Skyscrapers filled like water glasses
Great Lakes mixed with Buddhist brine
Great Books watered down in Evanston
Milwaukee beer topped with sea foam
Beau Fleuve of Buffalo suddenly become salt
Manhattan Island swept clean in sixteen seconds
buried masts of Amsterdam arise
as the great wave sweeps on Eastward
to wash away over-age Camembert Europe
Mannahatta steaming in sea-vines
the washed land awakes again to wilderness
the only sound a vast thrumming of crickets
a cry of seabirds high over
in empty eternity
as the Hudson retakes its thickets
and Indians reclaim their canoes

LOST PARENTS

It takes a fast car
                to lead a double life
in these days of short-distance love affairs
        when he has far-out lovers in
                        three different locations
        and a date with each one
                at least twice a week
a little simple arithmetic shows
        what a workout he's engaged in
crossing & recrossing the city
        from bedroom to patio to swimming pool
the ignition key hot
        and the backseat a jumble of clothes
                        for different life-styles
a surfboard on the roof
    and a copy of Kahlil Gibran or Rod McKuen
                        under the dashboard
        next to the Indian music casettes
packs of Tarot and the I-Ching
                crammed into the glove compartment
        along with old traffic tickets
                        and hardpacks of Kents
        dents attesting to the passion
                        of his last lover
And his answering service
        catching him on the freeway
                between two calls or two encounter groups
    and the urgent message left
        with an unlisted number to call Carol
        about the bottle of fine wine
            he forgot to pick up
                and deliver to the gallery
                    for the reception at nine

While she shuttles to her gynecologist
    and will meet him later
        between two other numbers
                male or female
  including his wife
      who also called twice
wanting to know where he's been
    and what he's done
          with their throw-away children
  who
      left to their own devices
        in a beach house at Malibu
  grew up and dropped out into Nothing
      in a Jungian search
           for lost parents
             their own age

PEOPLE GETTING DIVORCED

People getting divorced
        riding around with their clothes in the car
and wondering what happened
                to everyone and everything
               including their other
                       pair of shoes
     And if you spy one
        then who knows what happened
                to the other
                with tongue alack
and years later not even knowing
            if the other ever
                found a mate
           without splitting the seams
           or remained intact
                  unlaced

and the sole
        ah the soul
              a curious conception
      hanging on somehow
             to walk again
                in the free air
        once the heel
            has been replaced

SHORT STORY ON A PAINTING OF GUSTAV KLIMT

They are kneeling upright on a flowered bed
        He
                has just caught her there
                            and holds her still
            Her gown
                    has slipped down
                                off her shoulder
            He has an urgent hunger
                        His dark head
                                bends to hers
                                    hungrily
        And the woman the woman
            turns her tangerine lips from his
                one hand like the head of a dead swan
                    draped down over
                                his heavy neck
                        the fingers
                            strangely crimped
                                tightly together
            her other arm doubled up
                        against her tight breast
            her hand a languid claw
                            clutching his hand
        '   which would turn her mouth
                                            to his
            her long dress made
                    of multicolored blossoms
                        quilted on gold
            her Titian hair
                    with blue stars in it

And his gold
        harlequin robe
            checkered with
                dark squares
    Gold garlands
          stream down over
              her bare calves &
                tensed feet
Nearby there must be
        a jeweled tree
           with glass leaves aglitter
             in the gold air
It must be
      morning
          in a faraway place somewhere
They
    are silent together
            as in a flowered field
      upon the summer couch
           which must be hers
    And he holds her still
            so passionately
      holds her head to his
           so gently so insistently
      to make her turn
           her lips to his
Her eyes are closed
          like folded petals
She
    will not open
        He
         is not the One

THE 'MOVING WATERS' OF
GUSTAV KLIMT

Who are they then

these women in this painting

seen so deeply long ago

Models he slept with

or lovers or others

he came upon

catching them as they were

back then

dreamt sleepers

on moving waters

eyes wide open

purple hair streaming

over alabaster bodies

in lavender currents

Dark skein of hair blown back

from a darkened face

an arm flung out

a mouth half open

a hand

cupping its own breast

rapt dreamers

or stoned realists

drifting motionless

lost sisters or

women-in-love

with themselves or others—

17

pale bodies wrapt
in the night of women
lapt in light
in ground swells of
dreamt desire
dreamt delight

Still strangers to us
yet not
strangers
in that first night
in which we lose ourselves

And know each other

I AM YOU

M̲an half woman

Woman half man

And the two intertwined

in each of us androgynous

the limbs of one

around the limbs of the Other

clasping

my breast a vestigial remain

of yours

the heart a bivalve gasping

in a sea cave

(sound of sea waves lapping)

semen sea foam blown

into wombs of caves

thrown up

out of the body of being

out of the sea's mouth singing

(silent seabirds winging over)

                And the sea incarnadine

As Saint Matthew's Passion

      sung by a blind man

           comes over the Sunday morning radio

And I am alone here

      but if there were two of us

            I would say

There is only one here

      in the end as in beginning

          one body breathing

            one body singing

And the body is us

      the body is our selves

          and I am you

AT THE BODEGA

The hot young stud flamenco dancer
                              dressed like a bullfighter
       has fast feet like little animals
                     with their own identities
                     and a life of their own
              having nothing at all to do
                              with the rest of him
                     which watches
                              as they do the dancing
And each insolent gesture
                              which that body makes
       and each arrogant pose
                     that body takes
                              exactly like a toreador
       telling the woman he whirls around
              "I am your master
              You cannot touch me
              And in the end
              I will bring you
                     to my feet
                     with this
                              white handkerchief"

SNAPSHOT EPIPHANY

One night when it was very dark
    a certain Stephen appeared to me
                in an epiphany
                  in the Café Sport
   (that same Stephen no doubt named
     after Stephen Dedalus
       by that generation of parents
      who named all its children
      after the hero of
      Portrait of the Artist as a Young Man)
and that same Stephen coming up to me
    with a certain subversive air
         of an arab with a scarab
and showing me a color photo of himself
               in the Café Trieste
               three years ago
    looking like a young Pierre
       in the BBC version of *War & Peace*
and pointing out in a corner of the photo
       'the Greek chick I'm now involved with'
   whom he hadn't even met
          at the time of the picture
   ('The Greek *what?*' I asked him)

But there they were
         the two of them back then
   already 'caught in the emulsion'
       (as I pointed out to him)
  though the film not fully developed yet
         the final print not yet made
  the print in fact still to be
        put back in the developer

to bring out the darker shadowed parts
     of the total picture
in which his fated resemblance
    to a revolutionary Pierre
or to a liberated Stephen Dedalus
    would be made much much clearer
and her fatal resemblance
    to an Egyptian fertility goddess
      made much dearer

even as he strides forth to forge
    'the uncreated conscience of his race'
and even as he
    strode back to their table
and I spied her
   through the Italian lattice
     smiling so fatally at him
  and then kissing him
     gratis

OVERHEARD CONVERSATIONS

(In the U.S. Restaurant & Café Sport, San Francisco, Listening to Barlow Farrar, Tony Dingman & Others)

1.

A talent for eclectic theft
      when it came to stealing lines of poetry
           out of everybody's conversation
And Epictetus with a cactus
      couldn't have been more
           deadly with a dart
So that 'excrutia' becomes 'ex-Kruschev'
      (a Russian immigrant on the lamb)
  or another kind of Milquetoast
      with leftover spinach
           tacked to the wall
And the cardboard man in the next booth
      too 'aridite' to communicate
           with ordinary people
           with body odor
And still the whole idea of poetry being
      to take control of life
         out of the hands of
           the Terrible People

2.

And I always loved
      chance association
         she said

like a Chinese family playing mahjong
and at the same time listening to
                                    Keyboard Dave
                playing the piano blues
            at Minnie's Can-Do
nonchalant as a hairdresser
                watching an assassin with a scimitar
            decapitating a heart crane
                        (a bird with a heart-shaped head)
And Hart Crane discovering America
            (after his father invented the lifesaver)
                by jumping from the fantail of a freighter
                in the Caribbean—
                                    A pure
                                    terrorist act!

3.

Oh if only I could get
    my fourth-grade energy back
                                she told me
        instead of sleeping on cactus pillows
            under wall-hangings of
                children's blots from Nieman-Marcus
    and then waking up watching
                        Mean Joe Green on television
                    (a sort of Paul Bunyan front-lineman)
    Knock at your own risk
            and duck if you're in the way
        That's
            my philosophy
                        she tittered
                as two too cool young guys
                                    saunter in

and sit down at the next table
                smoking Luckies and looking around
                                without expression
         and it's Boredom City in their nook
            with nothing to do but scratch
And a
            Mexican song comes over the juke
                blotting out my childhood watching
                     bored groan-ups sitting around
                          like wet tortillas

4.

While I always dreamed of Afghanistan banana stands
      or of opening a roadhouse in Sante Fe
            serving blue cheese hamburgers
                garlic and scallions on English muffins
         with waitresses wearing cactus hats
            and electric Navajo blankets
      And couples in the booths
                     in the deep dream department
         holding each other's hands
                     like doves that might fly away
She the most
                mindless woman on earth
         and he
                (muy macho picchu)
                          a slob from the Avenues
      having almost as much fun as if
            they were home by themselves
                making love every half hour
                     for three days
                          and not going out much
                                after that

5.

And then in walks this zingy lady
   I hadn't seen in years
  And a strange sad face she had
         which I hardly recognized
    but she explained it—
        'It's three years later my dear
         and I've been in love
          a few times—
           my head in my cunt
             or close by'
And she really wanted
       the guy at the bar
         but had to leave
           without him
And the men laughed
    and said stuff in Italian
      which they always say
        when women leave bars

And polygamy a tiny village
          in Yucatan

6.

But I'm such an optimist
  the *idea* of the Blues
    always eluded me
  even when I met that
        black cattle rancher's wife
     who choked to death
        on a piece of steak

at a party in Santa Fe
while they were listening to
old 45's of Elmore James
who taught them how to treat a black woman
and how to see a black woman
like a new concept of the Blues

7.

When once freaked-out in Ixtlan
the Modesto of Mexico
after taking part in a
group grope
she took a Roar-shack test
while listening to the Ink Spots
and discovered watercolors
painting with her kerchoo tongue
dipped in Quechua ketchup
And one of the weird locals came up
and tried to get sexual again
but she demurred and stated
'Just because Omar Sharif
can play chess
doesn't mean he's Doctor Zhivago
wandering around with leaves
blowing in his face'
And at that very moment
two identical orders of nuns & monks
marched out of the adobe courtyard
chanting 'Liberation Through Masturbation'

8.

So back along the Ho Che Men Trail
with Mao or Mouth Say Tongue or Mouse Shoe Tongue

In the famous U.S. Restaurant
   in the last Golden Age of North Beach San Francisco
listening to mafioso conversations
   interlarded with hardrock wingding jabber
by Hong Kong longhair streetgang studs
   with their choppers idling outside
while right-on Red Guards give the finger to
   Chinatown American Legionnaires and sweatshop mothers
with Taiwan real estate men in sharkskin suits
   advancing up the boulevards
leading the Great Chinese Dragon on a string

And the ponderous Italian momma telling me
   "Da bossa no lika da doggie"
when my cockapoolie barked under the table
   at an unbound female foot
And one thousand plastic chopsticks
   dropped straight down thru the peeling ceiling
staking everybody out in their undies
   right where they sat

9.

And 'Tennis shoes!' said the seaman disgustedly
      'Tennis shoes! Like this here siren
                              marries the skipper
         and comes on board wearing tennis shoes
         and the crew is so quiet
                     you could hear a fish fart
      and the next thing you know
                     she's painting a tennis court
         on the after deck
            and stringing a net between the stanchions
      and then gets this pussy-whipped skipper
                  to throw tennis balls at her

which she bats back at him
                    with the Chinese cook playing ballboy
and then when we get out to sea
                    with a cargo of tennis balls bound for Wimbledon
                        on a sunny day between Scylla and Charybdis
                    she's batting balls like that
                        and slams one over the side
            and the racket goes over too
and she gets the skipper
                        to bring the ship about
            and put two men over the side
                            in a dinghy
to retrieve the floating capitalist racket
and the two men drown
            and the ship itself runs onto
                        a sawtooth reef
                and goes down with all hands
            as ten thousand tennis balls
                        bob to the surface'

10.

'Oh no—Onomatapoeia!'
                    cried the poetry workshop teacher
            when she didn't have to pee at all
                        in this Cafesportsevent
            when everyone got up
                        and just for a gas
            read their worst verse
                        (somewhat resembling this)
            —a random colloquial clapping
                            by one hand—
                ten poems burst from it
                            in one night
                tripping on one joint

And that was it
    and so 'Good Night Ladies'
         he then sang
   as he passed out naked
        (and really *hung*)
    into the adhesive arms
        and slung lips
   of the Strange One

THE HEAVY

There was this man who was not myself, this short, squat little man, this hunk of meat, this large toad of a man, sitting in the Trieste Café in San Francisco this Saturday noon, in the crowd that comes every Saturday to hear the *padrone* and his son and their friends sing Italian arias, sometimes to jukebox accompaniment and sometimes with a guest guitarist or blind mandolin player, and this noon there is this heavy, silent man sitting by himself at one of the little round tables, you could tell he was alone even though the table was surrounded with sitting people, jammed in, listening to the singing, and he had nothing in particular to attract me to him, he was obviously not attractive, even to women, and he sat there taking it all in, taking long drags on his very long thin *cigarillo*, and every once in a while taking a very small sip of his *cappuccino*, and they were into 'O Solo Mio' when I first noticed him and they were joined in the second chorus by a slender very lovely pale blond woman of maybe thirty-five or a questionable forty, who had a beautiful voice that soared up and away above the young crowd most of which wasn't locals but looked like they'd just come over for the morning on the Sausalito ferry, and this here heavy sitting there like a great hairy sloth or something, and drawing ever so slowly on his long *cigarillo*, holding the smoke so long it never came out anywhere and he so self-contained in the crowd, holding everything in, expressionless, yet watching the singers intently and listening with his large leaden ears which hung in straight black hair tinged with gray which looked like it might be glued to the bottom edge of his bright red felt fedora porkpie hat which he wore perfectly straight on his heavy head, this 'hat' with a life of its own on this head, with a hatband made of very small multi-colored feathers, as in a painting by Leonor Fini, and under this hat came the heavy lids over the heavy eyes behind the heavy lenses in the heavy horned-rims set on a soft-looking blunt nose, directly under which came the thick lips, on each side of which hung the heavy close-shaven jowls with black showing through the skin, and directly under the soft chin came a turtle throat, and then there was the buttoned-in gut in a white leather vest under which were bright red mod pants, and I leaned over and peered for the feet—new bulldog shoes with button hooks! and I contemplated chasing a coin or a hardboiled egg under the table to get a better look at this unbelievable hook-up but the blond singer was into "La Spagnola" and the whole place was humming with pure joy even though life itself was still a tragedy if you lay down, or at least a farce easily turned into a tragedy by sitting upon the ground, and "La Spagnola" proved it all, the sad sweet music pouring out of the lovely mouth of life itself, the parted lips of life, and one had the feeling that this heavy listener spent all his life sitting someplace watching everybody else's life go by, and that he would sit witnessing the most passionate acts of the most beautiful creatures, and show no reaction nor make the slightest gesture beyond the long dragging on his long *cigarillo,* and one could only wonder what bed or lover could possibly have borne him last night, and he was the Mafia godfather of Italian opera out on a scouting tour, and he was James Joyce's Artist, above, beyond, behind the scenes, indifferent, paring his fingernails, and he was a character in a corner of an Egyptian café in Lawrence Durrell's *Justine,* and he was Proust's solitary diner, and he was Dr. Matthew O'Connor in drag in Djuna Barnes' *Nightwood* asking "Watchman, what of the Night?" and he was watching everyone in his Night which was their day, for he was forever an exile in this lighted life, until suddenly a final golden solo came to a glorious climax and everyone clapped and laughed and untangled themselves and spilled out of the café laughing and talking, and the goldenhaired soprano who could have been a *contessa* went straight to *him* and bent over him and kissed him so fully on the lips that he rose up with the lips, and that man and that woman so close they floated out, into the sunlight, together!

GREAT AMERICAN WATERFRONT POEM

San Francisco land's end and ocean's beginning The land
the sea's edge also The river within us the sea about us The
place where the story ended the place where the story began
The first frontier the last frontier Beginning of end and end
of beginning End of land and land of beginning Embarcadero
Freeway to nowhere turned into part of Vaillancourt's
'Wrecked Freeway Fountain' What is the water saying to the
sea on San Francisco waterfront where I spent most of my
divorce from civilization in and out waterfront hangouts
China Basin Mission Rock Resort Public Fishing Pier Harbor
Lunch Tony's Bayview Red's Java House Shanty Gallery
Bottom-of-the-Mark Eagle Café Longshoreman's Hall the
Waterfront dead No Work No Pay Golden Gate Pilot Boat in
fog Podesta Divers SS American Racer rusty Mystic Mariner
Motorship Goy Mount Vernon Victory Red Stack Tugs standing out past the pier where I telephoned the lawyers saying I
was shipping out on the sailing ship Balclutha and wouldn't
be back until they tore down the Embarcadero Freeway along
with the rest of petroleum civilization and the literary-indus-
trial complex far from where I'm standing opposite Alcatraz
by the thousand fishing boats nested in green thick water The
sea a green god feeding Filipino fishermen on the quays Ha-
waiians in baseball caps and peajackets retired Chief Petty
officers casting live bait Puerto Ricans with pile-worms in
tincans Old capital N Negroes with catfish called something
else here The top of Angel Island showing through fog
funneled through Golden Gate Monday morning October sun
the Harbor Cruise boat tilting with tourists into a fogbank
Gulls on the roofs of piers asleep in sun The Last Mohican
eating his lunch out of a pail and catching his next lunch with
the last of it The phone booth where I telephoned It's All
Over Count Me Out The fog lifting the sun the sun burning

34

through The bright steamers standing out in the end of the first poem I ever wrote in San Francisco twenty years ago just married on a rooftop in North Beach overlooking this place I've come to in this life this waterfront of existence A great view and here comes more life The Western Pacific Freight Ferry ploughing across the horizon between two piers foghorn blowing as I ask a passing elderly ship captain in plaid suit and Tyrolean hat for the time and he takes out his pocket chronometer which says a quarter of two and tells me in thick Norwegian accent "Quarrter to Tvelve' he just off a plane from Chicago no doubt going to catch his ship for the Far East after visiting his aged mother in Minnesota Foghorns still sounding at the Golden Gate An old freighter light-in-the-water on headings adjusting its compass a pilot flag up and the captain on a wing of the bridge coffeemug in hand great-coat collar up The wind beginning to come up blowing the fog away from the phone booth the phone dial very clear All of Angel Island now visible through the fogbank A red hull appears standing-in loaded to the gunnels with oil An Arab on the bridge his turban flying Passing Alcatraz he buys it The Last of the Mohicans reels in his line On the end of it a string of beads once lost in a trade for Manhattan Island The Belt Line Railroad engine stands snorting on a spur next to the Eagle Café with a string of flats & boxcars I park on the tracks imbedded in asphalt and enter the Eagle Café a sign on the wall saying 'Save the Eagle—Last of an Endangered Species' and I get beer just as old brakeman runs in and shouts 'Blue Volkswagen bus!' I rush out and save my bus from the train I see a clock and run for the phone on the pier where the lawyer's supposed to call me back at noon There's a dude in the booth with his address book out and a lot of coins spread out on the ledge He's dialing ten numbers He's putting the coins in very slowly He starts talking slowly He's really enjoying himself The tide is running out The Balclutha strains at its moorings The guy in the booth has a lot to say

35

and lotsa time to say it He's in his own civilized world enclosed
in the booth of civilization and I'm in mine outside waiting
for my lawyer to call back with the final word on my divorce
from civilization Will they let Man be free or won't they Will
they or won't they let him be a barbarian or a wanderer if
he wants to I look at my reflection in the glass of the phone
booth outside It's like a mirror of the world with a wild me
in it and the Bank of America towering over behind me Will
Eros or Civilization win And who's this weirdo who is myself
and where does he think he's going to sail away to when
there isn't any longer any Away Another huge oiler stands
in All the fucked-up diplomats of the world on the bridge
holding empty champagne glasses as in a Fellini movie The
guy in the booth hangs up and falls out I sit down in the booth
and drink my beer waiting for the phone to ring The Balclutha's whistle blows The tide is at the ebb The phone rings

HIGHWAY PATROL

When we zoomed off Freeway 80 other side of Sacramento and fell into the Old West Motel Coffee Shoppe with the horseshoe entrance I was wearing my studded cowboy boots and Stetson hat and my big solid silver deputy star and I zapped down at the counter and ordered a big ole ranch breakfast like I could eat a horse and my side-kick he hollered for soup and fell back to the funky john where I left him in the stall hoping everything would come out alright heh-heh and bopped back to the counter past three old dingbats in a booth talking in some fuckin foreign accent about local real estate and I got my see-through coffee and the teenybop wait-ress served up the lukewarm soup and the ranch eggs and when my buddy escaped from the john he spooned up some of the lukewarm soup and po-litely noted how it tasted 'real weird' in fact it was burnt real bad which I pointed out to the half-ass fry-cook since the waitress had fled and this here cook comes worrying outa his hole in the wall and mumbles 'Sure as hell is burned, ye can smell it' and I says 'You sure as hell can, you ole fucker!' as I lit up a Marlboro with a wood match which I lit with my thumbnail and then we just whirled around on our stools and took out our po-lice magnums which we's supposed to carry even off-duty and let go with a few lil ole blasts right through the ceiling and like really woke that dump up and everybody got under the tables and started praying in Swedish or some other goddanged lingo and my buddy he sauntered up to the jukebox and punched in a couple selector buttons and give the machine a big jolt as I punched-in the fry-cook for good measure and the juke shakes all over and then blasts out so fuckin loud that the windows blew out and we got blasted right out the door and everybody come falling out after us and the box just keeps blasting and the holes in the ceiling we'd shot out is still smoking and sure as hell they catch fire and the juke itself catches fire with the Country Western singer still wailing away like as if his balls done got caught in the meatgrinder and it's Kell Robertson singing 'I Shot a Faggot in the Bathroom' and the local volunteer fire department comes sireening down the highway with antlers on the hood and busts right in with hard-on hoses and let the whole place have it with a bath of deer-blood spurting outa their big-ass hose but the fire kept blazing away in the jumping juke like a redhot potbelly stove about to blow up and the goddamn roof catches fire and everybody in sight freaks out and runs off down the road and over the hill outa sight Man we sure as hell lit that joint up if you know what I mean All good clean fun and we died laughin' Just like in the movies

SEASCAPE WITH SUN & EAGLE

Freer
           than most birds
     an eagle flies high up
                          over San Francisco
                              freer than most places
           soars high up
                     floats and glides high up
              in the still
                          open spaces

              flown from the mountains
                 floated down
                              far over ocean
                          where the sunset has begun
                          a mirror of itself

He sails high over
                          turning and turning
        where seaplanes might turn
           where warplanes might burn

     He wheels about burning
                              in the red sun
              climbs and glides
                          and doubles back
                                   upon himself
                 now over ocean
                              now over land
              high over pinwheels stuck in sand
                 where a rollercoaster used to stand

                       soaring eagle setting sun

All that is left of our wildness

DISSIDENTS, BIG SUR

January bright sun
tiny hummingbirds
in the willows
suddenly
flittering up

as an ordinary American monster
fourdoor sedan
barrels up the canyon road
backfiring & farting
carbon monoxide

And the hummingbirds take flight
in a flurry of fear
a cloud of them all at once
humming away
into deep blue air
where the sky sucks up
their wingéd hum
and in the infinite distance
eats them

Even as a crowd of huge defiant
upstart crows
sets up a ravening raucous
caw ! caw ! caw !

and screams and circles overhead
and pickets the polluted air
as the metal monster power-drives
on up the canyon
and over the horizon

And the crows now too
                    wing away on wind
    and are sucked up
               and disappear
                     into the omniverous universe

Even as any civilization
          ingests its own most dissident elements

ALIENATION: TWO BEES

I came upon them in the cabin—
　　the angry one at the window
　　　　and the old bent one on the bed
　　the one at the window buzzing & buzzing
　　　　　　beating its wings on the window
　　　　　　　　　beating the pane
　　the one on the bed
　　　　the silent one with the bent frame
　　　　　　　alone on the counterpane
I didn't mean to kill them
　　but the one in the window
　　　　　　　wouldn't be waved
　　　　　　　　back to his hive
　　The door was open and he knew it
　　　　and flew in it for a moment
　　　　and then flew back
　　　　　　　away from his community
Something had alienated him
　　　　and he would not go back
　　or was it perhaps
　　　　　　the wounded one on the bed
　　　　　　who kept him
I tried to get him to fasten onto
　　　　　a crumpled page
　　　　　　of the local news
　　　　but he would not
And I must have hurt him doing that
　　　　　for he fell on the bed
　　　　　　　and died in an instant
　　　stretching out his legs
　　　　　　　or arms

as if to his comrade or lover
who crawled a quarter-inch toward him
and then hunched up
into a very small furry ball
and was still
and would not move again
As all at once outside
the hive hummed louder
with a million mild conformists
with wild antennas bent

Not one flew out to wake the dead

No messenger was sent

A VAST CONFUSION

Long long I lay in the sands

Sound of trains in the surf
in subways of the sea
And an even greater undersound
of a vast confusion in the universe
a rumbling and a roaring
as of some enormous creature turning
under sea & earth
a billion sotto voices murmuring
a vast muttering
a swelling stuttering
in ocean's speakers
world's voice-box heard with ear to sand
a shocked echoing
a shocking shouting
of all life's voices lost in night
And the tape of it
somehow running backwards now
through the Moog Synthesizer of time
Chaos unscrambled
back to the first
harmonies

And the first light

OLBERS' PARADOX

And I heard the learned astronomer
    whose name was Heinrich Olbers
  speaking to us across the centuries
   about how he observed with naked eye
   how in the sky there were
     some few stars close up
  and the further away he looked
     the more of them there were
  with infinite numbers of clusters of stars
    in myriad Milky Ways & myriad nebulae

So that from this we may deduce
   that in the infinite distances
      there must be a place
      there *must* be a place
       where all is light
  and that the light from that high place
       where all is light
    simply hasn't got here yet
    which is why we still have night

But when at last that light arrives
   when at last it does get here
     the part of day we now call Night
     will have a white sky
      with little black dots in it
      little black holes
       where once were stars
And then in that symbolic
    so poetic place
      which will be ours
  we'll be our own true shadows
    and our own illumination
       on a sunset earth

UPON REFLECTION

Night's black mirror is broken

the star crab has scuttled away

with the inkwell

into India

Dawn

sows its mustard seed

In the steep ravines and gulches

of Big Sur

small animals stir

under the tough underbrush

as sun creeps down the canyon walls

into the narrow meadows

where the wild quail

run & cluck

Daytime moon

after much reflection says

Sun is God

And the stream

standing still

rushes forward

MATINAL

The critic crow

           struck by the song of

                        morning sun

        has his commentary to make

                     upon it

     stridently

             *

dear son

        do not wake

until I make

        this poem about it

Then rise & shine

          It

           is your world

DEEP CHESS

Life itself like championship chess
                    dark players jousting
        on a checkered field
                    where you have only
            so much time
                    to complete your moves
And your clock running
                    all the time
        and if you take
                    too much time
                        for one move
            you have that much less
                        for the rest
                of your life
And your opponent
                    dark or fair
            (which may or may not be
                        life itself)
        picking his nose or yours
        or bugging you with his deep eyes
        or obscenely wiggling his crazy eyebrows
        or blowing smoke in your face
            or crossing and recrossing his legs
                            or her legs
                to reveal a crotch
                    with or without balls
        or otherwise screwing around
            and acting like some insolent invulnerable
                            unbeatable god
            who can read your mind & heart

And one hasty move
                        may ruin you
        for you must play
                        deep chess
                (like the one deep game Spassky won from Fisher)

And if your unstudied opening
                                was not too brilliant
                you must play to win not draw
                        and suddenly come up with
                                a new Nabokov variation
And then lay Him out at last
                with some super end-game
                        no one has ever even dreamed of

And there's still time—
                        Your move

THE RECURRENT DREAM

One of those dreamed landscapes
                    you've dreamt over and over
        with a house you lived in
                    a long time ago
                            yet never existed
        and a causeway with a bridge
                    which in this latest version
                            has been taken down
        while you sit eating chocolate almonds
                            at a party
            in somebody's roofgarden
                        across the way
            and saying to someone
                        'I used to live
                            in that house
                                on the point'
        except that this time
                    the house itself
                        is gone
    And only the sea's noises
                    with the wood boats knocking
        keeps you from washing away

A RIVER STILL TO BE FOUND

Stoned &

singing Indian scat

with Ravi Shankar

(as if we knew him)

his sitar like a boat

by the 'river of life'

that flows on & on

into 'eternity'

Time itself a boat

upon that river

Slow distant figures

drawing barges

along those banks

the small drum a pulse

beating slow

under the skin

51

And our bodies

        still in time—

                transported—

     dreamt eternal

           by the Ganges—

                a river

           still to be found

           in the interior

            of America

MONET'S LILIES SHUDDERING

Monet never knew
               he was painting his 'Lilies' for
   a lady from the Chicago Art Institute
   who went to France and filmed
      today's lilies
         by the 'Bridge at Giverny'
               a leaf afloat among them
  the film of which now flickers
     at the entrance to his framed visions
      with a Debussy piano soundtrack
flooding with a new fluorescence (fleur-essence?)
   the rooms and rooms
              of waterlilies

Monet caught a Cloud in a Pond
                   in 1903
     and got a first glimpse
             of its lilies
   and for twenty years returned
     again and again to paint them
        which now gives us the impression
          that he floated thru life on them
                  and their reflections
    which he also didn't know
      we would have occasion
          to reflect upon

Anymore than he could know
      that John Cage would be playing a
         'Cello with Melody-driven Electronics'
           tonight at the University of Chicago
And making those Lilies shudder and shed
                 black light

INSURGENT MEXICO

In scorched dry desert

    where sun is god and god eats life

great god sun going down

    pastes up immense red posters

        on adobe walls

and then falls down

        over the horizon

      'with the flare of a furnace blast'

and the posters faded yellow

        fall into darkness

    leaving only shadows to prove

        one more revolution has passed

A MEETING OF EYES IN MEXICO

Suddenly
you are speaking to me
over the audience
as I speak my poem to it
My eyes encounter yours
over the crowd
Just a pair of eyes out there
in a far foto of faces
distant lamps
in a dark landscape
flickering
And the eyes speak—
in whatever tongue—
The poem ends
The eyes go on
burning
And there is applause out there
as on a dark sea
I hear it distantly
as in a sea shell—
shreds of sunlight blown—
As later your voice comes through—
in whatever tongue—
an impassioned questioning
of my poem—
I answer back
over the heads of the audience

I
    answer you
        Dark eyes
            speak to you
      over their heads
          Dark one
   'There is none
       like you
          among the dancers'

    Te amo

THE GENERAL SONG OF HUMANITY

On the coast of Chile where Neruda lived
   it's well known that
      seabirds often steal
           letters out of mailboxes
             which they would like to scan
             for various reasons
Shall I enumerate the reasons?
    They are quite clear
        even given the silence of birds
                on the subject
      (except when they speak of it
             among themselves
              between cries)
First of all
    they steal the letters because
        they sense that the General Song
           of the words of everyone
        hidden in these letters
      must certainly bear the keys
       to the heart itself of humanity
            which the birds themselves
              have never been able to fathom
      (in fact entertaining much doubt
        that there actually are
               hearts in humans)
And then these birds have a further feeling
      that their own general song
         might somehow be enriched
         by these strange cries of humans
     (What a weird bird-brain idea
       that our titterings might enlighten them)

But when they stole away
                with Neruda's own letters
            out of his mailbox at Isla Negra
        they were in fact stealing back
                    their own Canto General
    which he had originally gathered
                        from them
            with their omniverous & ecstatic
                        sweeping vision
But now that Neruda is dead
    no more such letters are written
        and they must play it by ear again—
            the high great song
                    in the heart of our blood & silence

Cuernavaca, October 26, '75

EIGHT PEOPLE ON A GOLF COURSE
AND ONE BIRD OF FREEDOM
FLYING OVER

The phoenix flies higher & higher
above eight elegant people on a golf course
who have their heads stuck in the sands
of a big trap
One man raises his head and shouts
I am President of Earth. I rule.
You elected me, heh-heh. Fore!
A second man raises his head.
I am King of the Car.
The car is my weapon. I drive all before me.
Ye shall have no other gods.
Watch out. I'm coming through.
A third raises his head out of the sand.
I run a religion. I am your spiritual head.
Never mind which religion.
I drive a long ball. Bow down and putt.
A fourth raises his head in the bunker.
I am the General. I have tanks to conquer deserts.
And my tank shall not want. I'm thirsty.
We play Rollerball. I love Arabs.
A fifth raises his head and opens his mouth.
I am Your Master's Voice.
I rule newsprint. I rule airwaves, long & short.
We bend minds. We make reality to order.
Mind Fuck Incorporated.
Satire becomes reality, reality satire.
Man the Cosmic Joke. Et cetera.
A sixth man raises his gold bald head.
I'm your friendly multinational banker.
I chew cigars rolled with petro-dollars.

59

We're above nations. We control the control.
I'll eat you all in the end.
I work on margins. Yours.
A woman raises her head higher than anyone.
I am the Little Woman. I'm the Tender Warrior
who votes like her husband. Who took my breasts.
A final figure rises, carrying all the clubs.
Stop or I'll shoot a hole-in-one.
I'm the Chief of All Police. I eat meat.
We know the enemy. You better believe it.
We're watching all you paranoids. Go ahead & laugh.
You're all in the computer. We've got all
your numbers. Except one
unidentified flying asshole.
On the radar screen.
Some dumb bird.
Every time I shoot it down
it rises.

POPULIST MANIFESTO

Poets, come out of your closets,
Open your windows, open your doors,
You have been holed-up too long
in your closed worlds.
Come down, come down
from your Russian Hills and Telegraph Hills,
your Beacon Hills and your Chapel Hills,
your Mount Analogues and Montparnasses,
down from your foot hills and mountains,
out of your tepees and domes.
The trees are still falling
and we'll to the woods no more.
No time now for sitting in them
As man burns down his own house
to roast his pig.
No more chanting Hare Krishna
while Rome burns.
San Francisco's burning,
Mayakovsky's Moscow's burning
the fossil-fuels of life.
Night & the Horse approaches
eating light, heat & power,
and the clouds have trousers.
No time now for the artist to hide
above, beyond, behind the scenes,
indifferent, paring his fingernails,
refining himself out of existence.
No time now for our little literary games,
no time now for our paranoias & hypochondrias,
no time now for fear & loathing,
time now only for light & love.

We have seen the best minds of our generation
destroyed by boredom at poetry readings.
Poetry isn't a secret society,
It isn't a temple either.
Secret words & chants won't do any longer.
The hour of *om*ing is over,
the time for keening come,
time for keening & rejoicing
over the coming end
of industrial civilization
which is bad for earth & Man.
Time now to face outward
in the full lotus position
with eyes wide open,
Time now to open your mouths
with a new open speech,
time now to communicate with all sentient beings,
All you 'Poets of the Cities'
hung in museums, including myself,
All you poet's poets writing poetry
about poetry,
All you poetry workshop poets
in the boondock heart of America,
All you house-broken Ezra Pounds,
All you far-out freaked-out cut-up poets,
All you pre-stressed Concrete poets,
All you cunnilingual poets,
All you pay-toilet poets groaning with graffitti,
All you A-train swingers who never swing on birches,
All you masters of the sawmill haiku
in the Siberias of America,
All you eyeless unrealists,
All you self-occulting supersurrealists,
All you bedroom visionaries
and closet agitpropagators,

All you Groucho Marxist poets
and leisure-class Comrades
who lie around all day
and talk about the workingclass proletariat,
All you Catholic anarchists of poetry,
All you Black Mountaineers of poetry,
All you Boston Brahmins and Bolinas bucolics,
All you den mothers of poetry,
All you zen brothers of poetry,
All you suicide lovers of poetry,
All you hairy professors of poesie,
All you poetry reviewers
drinking the blood of the poet,
All you Poetry Police—
Where are Whitman's wild children,
where the great voices speaking out
with a sense of sweetness and sublimity,
where the great new vision,
the great world-view,
the high prophetic song
of the immense earth
and all that sings in it
And our relation to it—
Poets, descend
to the street of the world once more
And open your minds & eyes
with the old visual delight,
Clear your throat and speak up,
Poetry is dead, long live poetry
with terrible eyes and buffalo strength.
Don't wait for the Revolution
or it'll happen without you,
Stop mumbling and speak out
with a new wide-open poetry
with a new commonsensual 'public surface'

with other subjective levels
or other subversive levels,
a tuning fork in the inner ear
to strike below the surface.
Of your own sweet Self still sing
yet utter 'the word en-masse'—
Poetry the common carrier
for the transportation of the public
to higher places
than other wheels can carry it.
Poetry still falls from the skies
into our streets still open.
They haven't put up the barricades, yet,
the streets still alive with faces,
lovely men & women still walking there,
still lovely creatures everywhere,
in the eyes of all the secret of all
still buried there,
Whitman's wild children still sleeping there,
Awake and walk in the open air.

BIBLIOGRAPHICAL NOTE

The publication history of "Populist Manifesto" is extraordinary: An early version was broadcast by the author on KPFA/FM (Berkeley) in April 1975. On April 23, he spoke it at Walt Whitman Day, Rutgers University (Camden). Its first appearance in print, like an early election return, was in a small town paper in New Hampshire, the *Granite State Independence* (Grantham, N.H.) in May 1975, followed closely by the Bolinas (California) *Hearsay News.* It was picked up by the *Los Angeles Times* on June 1, by *The New York Times* (Op/Ed page) on July 5, and by the *San Francisco Examiner* on August 10, 1975. (Apologies are due to the *American Poetry Review,* which had the poem set in type when it appeared in *The New York Times.*) A flood of publication in literary magazines followed: *The Chicago Review, California State Poetry Quarterly, Nitty Gritty* (Pasco, Washington), *Sol Tide* (New Mexico), and more informal mimeo places, since the author gave it to anyone who asked. . . . Within a half-year of its first publication, it also was translated into Spanish, Italian, French, and published in the anarchist *Antigruppo 1975* (Sicily) and *Impegno 70* (Sicily), and the *Revista de Bellas Artes* #23 (Mexico City). Its first publication in England was in *Z-revue Collective* (Leicester), and it was pirated in Yugoslavia. A broadside of it was printed by Vernon Chadwick Jr. at the Cranium Press (San Francisco) and reprinted later by City Lights Books. New Directions printed it in its anthology *ND31.* And the late jazz critic Ralph Gleason, in one of his last acts, wrote to Jann Wenner, editor of *Rolling Stone,* urging him to publish it as "an important literary document of the '70s." Thanks are due also to the following publications in which other poems herein first were printed: *The New York Times, Beatitude Magazine, Poetry*

65

Now, City of San Francisco, Los Angeles Times, San Francisco Examiner, Chicago Review, California State Poetry Quarterly, Revista de Bellas Artes, Transatlantic Review, San Francisco Bay Guardian, Bastard Angel, Pacific Sun Literary Quarterly, The CoEvolution Quarterly, and various *New Directions in Prose and Poetry* anthologies.

Some New Directions Paperbooks

Walter Abish, *Alphabetical Africa*. NDP375.
 In the Future Perfect. NDP440.
 Minds Meet. NDP387.
Ilangô Adigal, *Shilappadikaram*. NDP162.
Alain, *The Gods*. NDP382.
David Antin. *Talking at the Boundaries*. NDP388.
G. Apollinaire, *Selected Writings*.† NDP310.
Djuna Barnes, *Nightwood*. NDP98.
Charles Baudelaire, *Flowers of Evil*.† NDP71.
 Paris Spleen. NDP294.
Martin Bax. *The Hospital Ship*. NDP402.
Gottfried Benn, *Primal Vision*.† NDP322.
Jorge Luis Borges, *Labyrinths*. NDP186.
Jean-François Bory, *Once Again*. NDP256.
Kay Boyle, *Thirty Stories*. NDP62.
E. Brock, *The Blocked Heart*. NDP399.
 Here. Now. Always. NDP429.
 Invisibility Is The Art of Survival. NDP342.
 The Portraits & The Poses. NDP360.
Buddha, *The Dhammapada*. NDP188.
Frederick Busch, *Domestic Particulars*. NDP413.
 Manual Labor. NDP376.
Ernesto Cardenal, *Apocalypse & Other Poems*.
 NDP441.
 In Cuba. NDP377.
Hayden Carruth, *For You*. NDP298.
 From Snow and Rock, from Chaos. NDP349.
Louis-Ferdinand Céline,
 Death on the Installment Plan. NDP330.
 Guignol's Band. NDP278.
 Journey to the End of the Night. NDP84.
Jean Cocteau, *The Holy Terrors*. NDP212.
 The Infernal Machine. NDP235.
M. Cohen, *Monday Rhetoric*. NDP352.
Cid Corman, *Livingdying*. NDP289.
 Sun Rock Man. NDP318.
Gregory Corso, *Elegiac Feelings American*.
 NDP299.
 Happy Birthday of Death. NDP86.
 Long Live Man. NDP127.
Robert Creeley, *Hello*. NDP451.
Edward Dahlberg, *Reader*. NDP246.
 Because I Was Flesh. NDP227.
Osamu Dazai, *The Setting Sun*. NDP258.
 No Longer Human. NDP357.
Coleman Dowell, *Mrs. October . . .* NDP368.
 Too Much Flesh and Jabez. NDP447.
Robert Duncan, *Bending the Bow*. NDP255.
 The Opening of the Field. NDP356.
 Roots and Branches. NDP275.
Richard Eberhart, *Selected Poems*. NDP198.
Russell Edson, *The Falling Sickness*. NDP 389.
 The Very Thing That Happens. NDP137.
Wm. Empson, *7 Types of Ambiguity*. NDP204.
 Some Versions of Pastoral. NDP92.
Wm. Everson, *Man-Fate*. NDP369.
 The Residual Years. NDP263.
Lawrence Ferlinghetti, *Her*. NDP88.
 Back Roads to Far Places. NDP312.
 A Coney Island of the Mind. NDP74.
 The Mexican Night. NDP300.
 Open Eye, Open Heart. NDP361.
 Routines. NDP187.
 The Secret Meaning of Things. NDP268.
 Starting from San Francisco. NDP 220.
 Tyrannus Nix?. NDP288.
 Who Are We Now? NDP425.
F. Scott Fitzgerald, *The Crack-up*. NDP54.
Robert Fitzgerald, *Spring Shade*. NDP311.
Gustave Flaubert,
 The Dictionary of Accepted Ideas. NDP230.
M. K. Gandhi, *Gandhi on Non-Violence*.
 (ed. Thomas Merton) NDP197.
André Gide, *Dostoevsky*. NDP100.
Goethe, *Faust*, Part I.
 (MacIntyre translation) NDP70.
Albert J. Guerard, *Thomas Hardy*. NDP185.
Henry Hatfield, *Goethe*. NDP136.
John Hawkes, *The Beetle Leg*. NDP239.
 The Blood Oranges. NDP338.
 The Cannibal. NDP123.
 Death, Sleep & The Traveler. NDP393.
 The Innocent Party. NDP238.
 John Hawkes Symposium. NDP446.

The Lime Twig. NDP95.
 Lunar Landscapes. NDP274.
 The Owl. NDP443.
 Second Skin. NDP146.
 Travesty. NDP430.
A. Hayes, *A Wreath of Christmas Poems*.
 NDP347.
H.D., *Helen in Egypt*. NDP380
 Hermetic Definition NDP343.
 Trilogy. NDP362.
Robert E. Helbling, *Heinrich von Kleist*, NDP390.
Hermann Hesse, *Siddhartha*. NDP65.
C. Isherwood, *The Berlin Stories*. NDP134.
 Lions and Shadows. NDP435.
Philippe Jaccottet, *Seedtime*. NDP428.
Alfred Jarry, *The Supermale*. NDP426.
 Ubu Roi, NDP105.
Robinson Jeffers, *Cawdor and Medea*. NDP293.
James Joyce, *Stephen Hero*. NDP133.
 James Joyce/*Finnegans Wake*. NDP331.
Franz Kafka, *Amerika*. NDP117.
Bob Kaufman,
 Solitudes Crowded with Loneliness. NDP199.
Hugh Kenner, *Wyndham Lewis*. NDP167.
Kenyon Critics, *Gerard Manley Hopkins*.
 NDP355.
P. Lal, *Great Sanskrit Plays*. NDP142.
Tommaso Landolfi,
 Gogol's Wife and Other Stories. NDP155.
Lautréamont, *Maldoror*. NDP207.
Irving Layton, *Selected Poems*. NDP431.
Denise Levertov, *Footprints*. NDP344.
 The Freeing of the Dust. NDP401.
 The Jacob's Ladder. NDP112.
 O Taste and See. NDP149.
 The Poet in the World. NDP363.
 Relearning the Alphabet. NDP290.
 The Sorrow Dance. NDP222.
 To Stay Alive. NDP325.
 With Eyes at the Back of Our Heads.
 NDP229.
Harry Levin, *James Joyce*. NDP87.
Enrique Lihn, *The Dark Room*. NDP452.
García Lorca, *Five Plays*. NDP232.
 Selected Poems.† NDP114.
 Three Tragedies. NDP52.
Michael McClure, *Gorf*. NDP416.
 Antechamber. NDP455.
 Jaguar Skies. NDP400.
 September Blackberries. NDP370.
Carson McCullers, *The Member of the
 Wedding*. (Playscript) NDP153.
Thomas Merton, *Asian Journal*. NDP394.
 Gandhi on Non-Violence. NDP197.
 The Geography of Lograire. NDP283.
 My Argument with the Gestapo. NDP403.
 New Seeds of Contemplation. NDP337.
 Raids on the Unspeakable. NDP213.
 Selected Poems. NDP85.
 The Way of Chuang Tzu. NDP276.
 The Wisdom of the Desert. NDP295.
 Zen and the Birds of Appetite. NDP261.
Henri Michaux, *Selected Writings*.† NDP264.
Henry Miller, *The Air-Conditioned Nightmare*.
 NDP302.
 *Big Sur & The Oranges of Hieronymus
 Bosch*. NDP161.
 The Books in My Life. NDP280.
 The Colossus of Maroussi. NDP75.
 The Cosmological Eye. NDP109.
 Henry Miller on Writing. NDP151.
 The Henry Miller Reader. NDP269.
 Remember to Remember. NDP111.
 The Smile at the Foot of the Ladder. NDP386.
 Stand Still Like the Hummingbird. NDP236.
 The Time of the Assassins. NDP115.
 The Wisdom of the Heart. NDP94.
Y. Mishima, *Confessions of a Mask*. NDP253.
 Death in Midsummer. NDP215.
Eugenio Montale, *New Poems*. NDP410.
 Selected Poems.† NDP193.
Vladimir Nabokov, *Nikolai Gogol*. NDP78.
 The Real Life of Sebastian Knight. NDP432.
P. Neruda, *The Captain's Verses*.† NDP345.
 Residence on Earth.† NDP340.

Complete descriptive catalog available free on request from
New Directions, 333 Sixth Avenue, New York 10014.   † Bilingual